WOMEN WHO FINISH

THE TAKE-ACTION WORKBOOK

for Getting Past Procrastination and

Perfectionism to Get Things Done.

INCLUDES A 90 DAY GOAL PLANNER

ROBYN-ANN YOUNG

"Brothers and sisters, I do not consider myself yet to have taken hold of it. But one thing I do: Forgetting what is behind and straining toward what is ahead, **I press on toward the goal to win** the prize for which God has called me..."

– Philippians 3:13-14

WHAT'S INSIDE?

WELCOME

INTRODUCTION

Hello lionheart!

Welcome to the Women Who Finish squad.

I created this workbook to help virtuous women like you finally take hold of all the plans calling to you from your purpose... all the promises that Jesus died for... all the passions that have been blazing in your heart.

Why? Because not finishing your own race has been draining your confidence, clarity, & creativity. I know, because I've been there.

Like myself, you've seen many years pass where you began with a ton of inspiration and good intentions, but ended with no implementation to show for it.

While mentoring* over the past ten years, I noticed that most women knew what they wanted out of life – but would carelessly settle into habits that sabotaged and contradicted their true desires.

Of course, no one does this intentionally. However, we compromise when we overlook the day-to-day choices that are actually important to get us to the end.

We often get caught up in the emotions of a fresh start, a fresh idea, or the fresh smell of a brand new journal. Only to realize that finishing requires so much more: clear strategy and mindset shifts which I've had to learn the hard way – and will be sharing with you.

God's grace is sufficient beloved. So let's renew our mind and finish what He's started in us.

– Robyn-Ann

*To learn more or to access the mastermind support that complements these modules, be sure to visit WomenWhoFinish.com

GET WHAT YOU REALLY CAME FOR

MODULE 1

PROBE YOUR PASSIONS

PROBE YOUR PASSIONS

It's time to get honest about your passions and what you ultimately desire beloved. That's the only way to get motivated enough to give up what you want now (ease, excuses, comfort, perfect scenarios) for what you want most (results, transformation, progress, change).

When you don't acknowledge your passions, you don't give yourself a reason to obsess over the things God made you to get excited about. Which means, you keep waiting for someone else to validate that fire in your heart.

However, no one else was built with that same calling, so no one else can see what you see. You have to decide that God gave YOU the vision, so you will have to pursue it alone at first.

And yes, it will take everything that you've got – but you've got everything that it will take to get there. IF you own it as YOUR passion.

Because without passion, you don't give yourself permission to persevere past the pain that's holding you back right now.

So you have to get in touch with today's pain and realize that it's nothing compared to the promise of God currently nagging at your heart. Your fear and excuses are not worth abandoning the issues you were created to solve.

Yes, there will always be challenges – but you must choose the pain of pressing towards your goals rather than the pain of regret and procrastination.

We often tell ourselves that we're okay where we are right now.

But are you really?

Once you take a deeper look, you will realize that you've just made excuses for settling down in the comfort zone. And that coasting on the status quo is nothing but life support – since you're not really alive or breathing for yourself.

That's why we're about to stir up the flame of what you really came for... the fire that Jesus died for. And just commit to it.

Yes, it will take time, but time will fly anyway. Your job is deciding whether you will be the pilot of your own time, or whether your boss and church be?

Get so obsessed with your calling that you finally obey your thirst for greater.

You must be able to see, feel, and imagine the end point and the pleasure it will bring – as well as the pain it will relieve. For that's how you constantly remind yourself that discipline will hurt way less than regret.

Answer the following questions to dig up the frustrations and fears that you've been suppressing and deal with them. They are not that big once you take them before a Mighty God.

MODULE 1 MINDSET SHIFTS:

What do I really want MORE THAN ANYTHING?

Why do I really want this?

What root desire will it satisfy?

What don't I want for sure? Why is that?

Where do I want to end up one year from now?

Why is it so important to end up there?

What frustrations will I feel if this is not accomplished?

Which excuses do I usually come up with to put this off?

Are any of these excuses valid?

Are there temporary solutions that can get me going until perfect comes?

How has this project been sabotaged in the past?

If I was the enemy, how would I attack myself again to keep me stuck?

How will I respond differently this time?

FLASH FORWARD – QUESTIONS:

It's one year from now, how do I feel having achieved this goal?

Which new freedoms has it allowed me to have?

Who am I now able to serve with these passions?

What are friends and family now saying about my strong focus and finish?

Were the pain and tears worth it?

HOW HAS FINALLY WALKING IN MY PURPOSE BENEFITED & AFFECTED:

- Me Personally?

- My Family?

- My Children & Grandchildren? (it's that deep)

- My Friendships?

- My Generation?

FUEL TO FINISH

"For I consider that the sufferings of this present time are not worth comparing with the glory that is to be revealed in us."

– Romans 8:18

"Hope deferred makes the heart sick, but a desire fulfilled is a tree of life."

– Proverbs 13:12

The Take Action Workbook

ON TO THE NEXT ONE

MODULE **2**

PINPOINT YOUR FOCUS

PINPOINT YOUR FOCUS

Ok lionheart, it's time to identify the straightest path to your ultimate goal and where you should start. Because finishing one thing is better than just starting ten. Amen? Amen.

So we're not about to pursue twenty resolutions in the same season. Nobody has the time or energy for that.

I'm sure you've already tried that at some point in the past, and have failed miserably. That's possibly why you're reading this today! Indeed, you've witnessed that trying to re-haul your entire life at once never works.

A savvy woman of God knows how to count the cost and only build a house that's sized based on the resources she currently has.

We can do all things through Christ, but we cannot do them all at once.

That's why completing the journey of a thousand miles happens by placing one step firmly at a time – not by breaking your legs trying to jump one mile ahead with a single move.

Focus on arriving at the stepping stone directly in front of you, and it will automatically advance you and make getting to the next stepping stone easier. Dominating your dreams will start by conquering just one goal in the beginning. This is how you develop a stronger mindset that has a much better chance of finishing.

Purpose-driven women must know how to zoom in to the most pressing action that will make the most difference right now. Because once they excel in that one area, it then cultivates confidence to move on to the next project aggressively.

Therefore, let's switch your mindset to **completing** one important resolution. Pinpoint the one thing that you really want – the one change that's really going to help these other doors open up.

Recognize that your limited time, energy, and willpower is a good thing. No really, it is!

You've been designed that way in God's wisdom to help you focus and fully enjoy one thing. Don't worry, putting all your grit into one purpose for this season will guarantee that it actually succeeds. Which means, before you know it, you'll be done and already moving on to the next big thing.

But first, focus.

MODULE **2** MINDSET SHIFTS:

Which of the passions recognized from MODULE 1 would be the biggest stress reliever?

Which one would be the quickest to tackle?

Which venture would be the hardest?

Which focus would give me the most confidence to complete the others once finished?

Which goal is foundational to the others being able to take off?

Choose ONE passion to focus on based on the previous answers. Now answer these questions below to determine where to start:

Within this passion, which tasks do I feel the most ready to execute?

Which project am I most burning to produce?

Which tasks can be knocked out in a quarter? A month? A week?

Which tasks would create the biggest return in my business or self-esteem?

Which one would create actual monetary profit?

Which one would ease the pain?

Which tasks are most affordable right now?

Which have I been putting off the longest?

Is there friend who can help me launch one of these?

Can I barter or exchange services instead of money to get one of these done sooner/cheaper?

FUEL TO FINISH

"Do not despise these small beginnings, for the LORD rejoices to see the work begin..."

– Zechariah 4:10

"If you are faithful in little things, you will be faithful in large ones. But if you are dishonest in little things, you won't be honest with greater responsibilities."

– Luke 16:10

I WOKE UP LIKE THIS

MODULE **3**

PREPARE YOUR MENTAL SPACE

PREPARE YOUR MENTAL & PHYSICAL SPACE

Working on your goals does not happen in a vacuum, so you have to prepare your atmosphere for success. As I'm sure you know all too well, there will be an unlimited demand for your attention and endless requests for you to show up to "mandatory" events. But you cannot allow the urgent to trump what's important.

Only you can prioritize your purpose.

And saying yes to your calling means you'll have to start saying no to everyone else's. Yep, surprise, surprise! You can't work to please God and please people at the same time.

So let's clean out the mental and physical distractions that always keep you busy but unproductive in your passions.

To do this, a clear mind and a clear space is essential. Purpose-driven women setup healthy boundaries to guarantee that they'll act without getting in their own way.

That way, you can get up and just go because you've already made your decisions upfront, and simplified your commitments. Which means you're not wasting time in the moment overanalyzing preferences that don't really advance progress. Your thought patterns, tools and strategies need to be on autopilot so you can easily act on what's important without overthinking.

Because the reality is, if you're overthinking, you're underperforming.

For example, you want to know beforehand where you're going to show up to work productively. Establish the specific wardrobe you'll put on the night before or simplify it for the mornings. Strip down your diet and meals to a basic routine. Also, know what time you'll be in bed and what time you'll be make your way home from events to keep that rest commitment to yourself.

This is not a joke. I still assign myself a strict curfew and have no apologies about it; because how I spend my night, is how I'll spend my morning. And even further, how I spend each day is how I ultimately spend my life. The same applies to you.

You can either be rushed and regretful, or rested and ready. You choose beloved.

Review the following questions to help you prepare your mental and physical space on weekends (or in dedicated decision making slots on your calendar). That way, when it's time to execute, you're able to move with clarity, conviction, and consistency.

Stop grinding and start optimizing. Success has to start from the night before so you wake up ON.

Let's work smarter.

MODULE 3 MINDSET SHIFTS:

Is everything available, accessible, and ready to go for me to succeed in this?

How can I set myself up to just do without thinking?

Where specifically will I do this work?

Has this spot worked for me in the past?

How will I distract-proof it?

How can I further clear my mind to give this my all?

Which excuses can I no longer afford to entertain or muse over?

Which promises from God should I meditate on to stay focused?

What other projects can I pause right now to focus on getting this done?

People who succeed in doing this frequently, where do they work?

Is there any way I can get around those groups of people?

How will I keep notifications on my phone from distracting me?

How will I ensure that I don't spend the money set aside for this?

FUEL TO FINISH

"Therefore, since we are surrounded by such a great cloud of witnesses, let us **throw off everything that hinders...** And let us run with perseverance the race marked out for us."

– Hebrews 12:1-2

"For am I now seeking the approval of man, or of God? Or am I trying to please man? If I were still trying to please man, I would not be a servant of Christ."

– Galatians 1:10

PERFECTIONISM CAN'T SIT WITH US

MODULE **4**

PRIORITIZE YOUR TASKS

PRIORITIZE YOUR TASKS

Ready to dive into your to-do lists gorgeous? Good! However, we first have to face an ugly truth:

All tasks are not created equal.

It's true. Just because you write down 20 things that you would love to get done today does not mean they are going to happen.

And that is because your brain can't prioritize 20 things at the same time. As a result, since your brain knows it won't be able to complete such a tall order, it usually gets overwhelmed or shuts down before you can even make substantial progress towards your goals.

Well, what's the solution to this?! I'm glad you asked!

We're going to cut all the perfectionist fluff suffocating your brain, and put no more than 2-3 priorities on your to-do list for each day.

Of course, there are many things you could do to carry out this project. But then, there are the things that you must do. Big difference. And you have to differentiate the two when training your brain to finish each day's focus.

Creating an extensive to-do list of priorities only invites perfectionism and procrastination to your "get it done!" party. Which nobody wants, because they're the mean girls that just show up to poop and whine about everything that's happening.

So we're not here to make friends with perfection, but to protect progress.

Perfectionism and procrastination will continually try to sneak in to the party to sabotage progress, but you are here to protect progress with your life. It's your very purpose and the reason you're breathing today.

Don't let purpose get kidnapped by these evil twins. They are good for nothing and always up to no good. And they've taken many dreams to the grave empty-handed, with no legacy to leave behind.

Be on guard.

Review the following questions to help you establish the items that are essential to getting this project done. Then list these items as the main target and to do for each week. Anything else is just bonus – and only attended to once the required tasks are completed.

Trust me, you'll get more done by focusing on less.

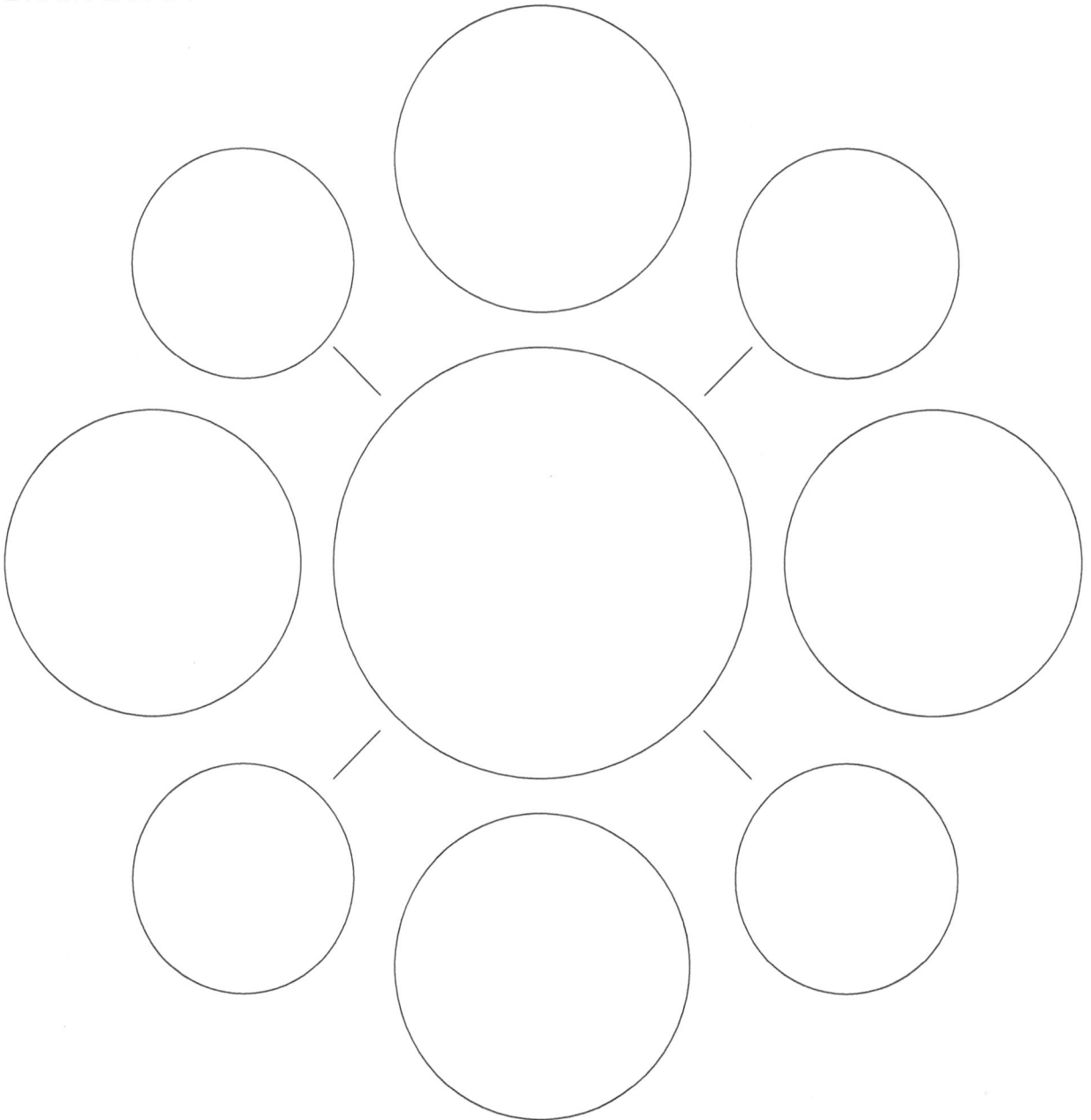

MODULE **4** MINDSET SHIFTS:

Do a brain dump of everything you feel needs to be done to complete this project, then ask yourself the following questions.

BRAIN DUMP:

Does everything on this list absolutely have to get done to succeed?

If I had to launch it imperfectly ASAP, which items would I cut out?

If someone offered me $100,000 to complete this project tomorrow, which 3 items would I prioritize?

How can I switch my goal from fancy to functional so that people waiting for what I offer can start benefiting sooner rather than later? (ie. get a $5 logo from Fiverr.com instead of waiting to save up for a graphic designer)

Now that the general requirements for finishing have been stripped down, remember to assign no more than 3 tasks per day to finish consistently and realistically.

FUEL TO FINISH

"But don't begin until you count the cost. For who would begin construction of a building without first calculating the cost to see if there is enough to finish it?"

– Luke 14:28

"Pay careful attention, then, to how you walk, not as unwise but as wise, making the best use of the time..."

– Ephesians 5:15-16

DON'T LIE TO YOURSELF

MODULE **5**

PLAN YOUR SCHEDULE

PLAN YOUR SCHEDULE

If you plan to get nowhere, that's where you'll end up... it's a common saying. Yet many of us still avoid using a personal calendar, and wonder why we aren't seeing consistent progress.

Because success is what you do intentionally over a long period of time. It's not just based on Sunday prayers and random spurts of action. To create a lifestyle of discipline, you need a long-term strategy.

Let's plan your work so you can work your plan.

If the prioritized tasks from MODULE 4 have not been assigned a specific slot on your calendar, then that means they do not exist. Yes, I'm sure you're confident you'll do them someday. However, someday will never come because it is not a day of the week.

Someday is only a figment of your imagination, and it's time you stop talking to imaginary friends.

Don't lie to yourself beloved. I don't like when others lie to me, so I don't lie to myself either. I put things that are important to me on an exclusive slot in my calendar so it has a sure place in my future that I must encounter and meet. And you must do the same.

Planning your schedule forces you to avoid the good to make time for the great.

Planning is also essential because it helps you realize what you can no longer afford to do or entertain. You cannot expect to have the same friendships, the same relationships, the same habits, the same excuses and think you're going to put out different results this year.

Things in your routine must change, or else nothing changes.

Cut out any fluff so you don't get overwhelmed and sidetracked by inconsequential tasks.

Break every single task down – to the minute if necessary.

Based on your end goal, and prioritized tasks, you should know what you need to do each week to make progress, and what you will be doing each day. Answer the following questions to help you work backward on your goals, and schedule each step on a clear timeline.

MODULE **5** MINDSET SHIFTS:

Based on my overall target result, how long will it take to achieve?

How many weeks total do I have to make this happen?
This is (x).

Now break down the desired outcome/results into (x) amount of chunks, to know how much progress to measure for each week:

Then take each weekly chunk and break it up into daily bits. What EXACLTY will I do daily to make measurable progress?

Which days will I work on these EXACT steps?

What EXACT time will I work on each of those EXACT days?

Is each task written out on their assigned day in my calendar? (Use the 90 day planner at the end of the book to map it all out if nothing else.)

Do I have anything else assigned in those slots that could distract me?

Have I allotted for time to travel to a dedicated space where I can get in the zone alone or around other grinders (whichever setting makes me the most productive) and work unbothered?

Have I allowed extra buffer time just to make sure I still get it done even if I meet upon challenges?

FUEL TO FINISH

"Teach us to number our days, that we may gain a heart of wisdom."

– Psalm 90:12

"Give careful thought to the paths for your feet and be steadfast in all your ways. Do not turn to the right or the left..."

– Proverbs 4:26-27

THESE FEELINGS AIN'T LOYAL

MODULE **6**

PARTNER WITH OTHERS

PARTNER WITH OTHERS

You have your plan, and clear priorities – and you're ready to run your excuses over with consistent action. Because action cures fear. And, of course, purpose doesn't work unless you do.

However, that doesn't mean that your emotions will always feel this way.

Until this discipline to finish becomes an effortless habit (which takes at least 21 consistent days to establish anew), you'll want to quit-proof your agenda by getting people involved.

No matter how motivated you feel right now, you aren't superwoman so you will have low days: laziness, lack of drive, feeling like a loser, etc. It's inevitable, so it's nothing to be ashamed of or fearful about.

Yet, a disciplined woman doesn't allow low days to hijack her purpose.

She know that feelings aren't loyal so she can't be loyal to them either. And as a result, she puts systems in place to check her before quitting even becomes an option.

Women who finish already know to collaborate with other individuals, set up accountability, get in a mastermind or sign up for a coach to keep her progress preserved against the tide of her moods.

Because feelings fade, but results are forever.

So successful women are just smart enough to work together and protect their plans from their own inconsistent selves. And you are no different beloved.

You can now learn to switch to your future self and operate from her successful mindset. You now think like she thinks, and move like she moves – which is confident, competent, and consistent. She doesn't need to like the people who keep her accountable, they just need to be awesome at keeping her excellent and excuse-free.

Because again, this call on your life is so much bigger than you.

Let's review the following journal prompts to establish some healthy relationships that align with where you want to go. That way you become so addicted to seeing results that you will immediately develop allergies towards your own excuses.

MODULE **6** MINDSET SHIFTS:

Do I have a fellow purpose-driven peer that I can ask to meet up with each week for work accountability?

When will I reach out to them?

As a backup, who is another go-getting friend that I can ask to check in with me and track my progress?

If the above two people fall through, can I find a mastermind online to join and get put in the hot seat for producing results?

If all else fails, who is another successful women that I've noticed at my church or job that I can ask for mentorship?

Am I willing to invest in a business or life coach to guarantee results if the above methods aren't keeping me consistent?

****Shameless Plug: Check out the Women Who Finish monthly mastermind to squad up with other virtuous women committed to finishing their calling and God-given race. Sign up for the next cycle or find out more details at: **WomenWhoFinish.com**

FUEL TO FINISH

"If either of them falls down, one can help the other up. But pity anyone who falls and has no one to help them up."

– Ecclesiastes 4:10

"Plans fail for lack of counsel, but with many advisers they succeed."

– Proverbs 15:22

ALL I DO IS WIN WIN WIN

MODULE **7**

PROCESS THROUGH ROADBLOCKS

PROCESS THROUGH ROADBLOCKS

Now, just because you have a plan doesn't mean that things will go as planned. Actually, I'll let you in on an important secret: things never do.

And that's okay. Women who finish plan for that too :)

Why do you think God wired grace into the system? Because He is the one who permits challenges and changes – to stretch us and sharpen our character. After all, Jesus doesn't just care about what we're doing. He mainly cares about who we're becoming. And because of that, heaven's not nervous about the obstacles that are up ahead but uses each hurdle to train us for the next level. So you don't need to be nervous either.

It doesn't get easier, but you get better.

Nothing worth finishing has ever been completed painlessly without some resistance. From Jesus' journey to the cross, to your mother birthing you into this world – purpose is usually produced through pain and perseverance.

Therefore, your race is no exception. There will be some friction, frustration, and even failure.

However, what seems like failure is just success in motion.

We serve a God that is working all things out for our good, and will change any loss into a win for His name's sake. And that's the awesome thing about doing things that align with God's kingdom agenda. His plans are going to get carried out no matter what. So we just have to stick with the winning team, and He'll guarantee our victory – even if we drop a few balls.

Once you have that solution-mindset renewed in Christ, problems just become miracles waiting to be unwrapped. You serve a God whose job begins at impossible, remember? (Matthew 19:26) Therefore, anything causing you to feel stuck is just an invitation to ask for some clear wisdom as James 1:5 tells us.

Don't abort God's call on your life because YOU don't know what to do. This is not about you.

This was never about you beloved.

The vision you carry is from God's infinite heart, so it needs God's infinite mind to succeed. Lean into Him and draw the solutions necessary to give Him glory in this endeavor. Because the righteous shall live by faith, and faith alone. So when working on kingdom projects, you don't get to be a know-it-all who did this in your own effort.

No, we are not self-made women.

We operate by the Holy Spirit and the supernatural help that He already has stored up for us.

Let's take a hold of His strength and win!

MODULE 7 MINDSET SHIFTS:

What are some areas of need causing me to hesitate or harbor anxiety when pursuing this project?

Have I asked God for supernatural help and specific help on it?

Is my worry being fed by things I believe I'll need down the road, even though the journey hasn't taken me there yet?

Has God provided enough for me to get started with what I have now?

Can I barter or trade any of my current possessions or services to get started?

Could I think of substitute resources if I were a single mom who had to make a way to do this and feed my child?

If I lost my job and became homeless tomorrow, which God-given skills and experience would I hustle to bring in some funds to get this off the ground?

Has anyone launched this project with less than I have? Be honest.

Have I asked God for His supernatural wisdom to create the solution this problem needs?

FUEL TO FINISH

Jesus said to him, "No one who puts his hand to the plow and looks back is fit for the kingdom of God."

– Luke 9:62

If any of you lacks wisdom, you should ask God, who gives generously to all without finding fault, and it will be given to you.

– James 1:5

PLEASE DON'T KILL MY SHINE

MODULE **8**

PUBLISH YOUR PROJECT

PUBLISH YOUR PROJECT

Yes lionheart! You have pushed past the resistance, kept swimming and smashed all your steps. Now it's time to boldly proclaim what God has given you to share.

Because again, this was never about us. Our gifts, ideas, and talents are birthed from the Holy Spirit's desire to bless people and bring heaven to earth.

So there's no use finishing something just to bury it under a bushel and hope someone will notice it if God reaaaally wants them to. *side eye*

Don't laugh, we have a tendency to do this as Christian women. We'll setup the blog, publish the posts, and then keep it a secret for the internet to stumble upon if the wind blows them by. Or we'll finally compile that recipe book but keep it stored in Microsoft Word for that "one day" when we get discovered by a publisher or can afford a big time TV launch.

I wrote the Women Who Finish devotional in one day earlier in 2015, then had it sitting on Dropbox for months. I told myself that I was waiting to figure out how to do the perfect book launch. Like errr...? Why do we do this?!

Let's stop the madness and false humility.

True humility means being radically obedient to excel in everything that God has asked you to do, say, or create.

Therefore, in the same way God expects you to steward your talents, He also expects you to properly package and position it in front of an audience. That way you get a worthy return on your investment (which is really His investment of the skills and time He gave you, let's not forget).

This is so much bigger than you and I beloved.

I mean, Jesus didn't call you the light of the world as a joke.

You have been set apart to shine. This is the identity and behavior He expects us to carry out as His ambassadors and representatives.

This is how you shine, by loudly sharing what you have with the world! Own up to what you accomplished and promote it shamelessly to those who could benefit.

Be so good at marketing the value that God has deposited inside of you, that everyone in your sphere of influence experiences a breakthrough in that area.

Market your gifts with all of your heart and let's roar.

MODULE 8 MINDSET SHIFTS:

Have I announced my finished project to anyone?

Did I promote my new creation on my social media and web pages?

IF IT'S A PERSONAL GOAL:

Have I documented all the steps and strategies used to conquer – in case I need to do this challenge again or help someone else going forward?

Have I asked anyone to celebrate with me?

IF IT'S A PRODUCT:

Have I positioned it in front of the people who really need it?

Have I done a tutorial so people get to see it in action?

Have I clearly showcased its value and how it will positively change the lives of the users in practical ways? (Focus on the practical benefits and solutions people are looking for, not just the theoretical features).

IF IT'S A SERVICE:

Have I priced my genius and offered it in diverse formats so various people can access it? (ie. turn higher priced makeup services into a lower-priced video online course for those who cannot yet afford to hire me one-on-one)

Is it clearly visible how people can get in contact with me to enjoy my new offerings?

FUEL TO FINISH

"In the same way, let your light shine before others, so that they may see your good works and give glory to your Father who is in heaven."

– Matthew 5:16

"...But the righteous are bold as a lion."

– Proverbs 28:1

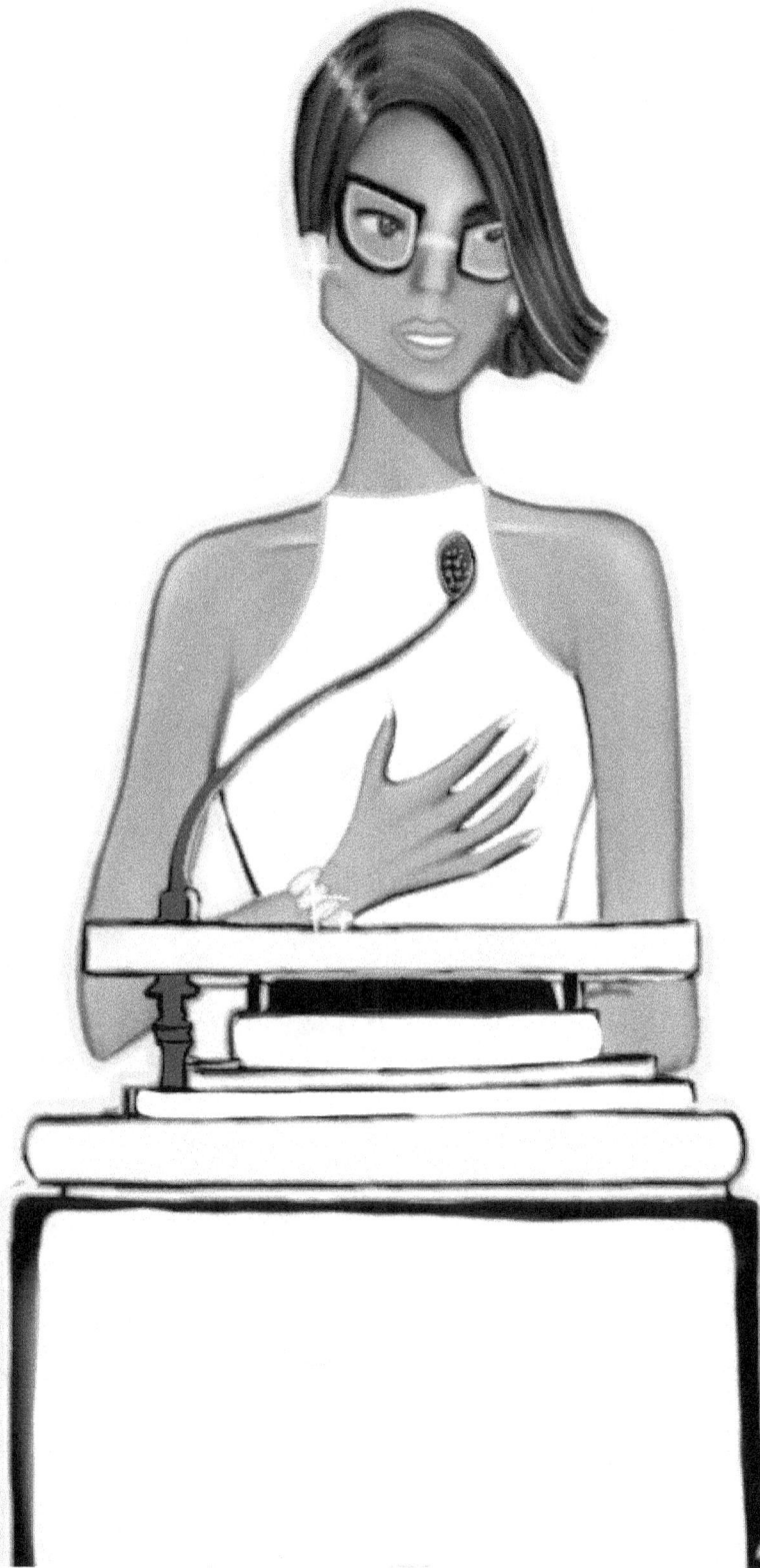

TURN ALL THE WAY UP

MODULE **9**

POP THE BUBBLY

POP THE BUBBLY

No, this is not an accidental add on.

I'm serious. One of the keys to self-discipline and staying motivated is knowing how to celebrate your wins – big and small. And I don't just mean the casual "Well, I'm glad that's done."

You cultivate true joy and appreciation for your progress when you give yourself permission to get really excited about what you've accomplished. Because this is a milestone that many only dream of, and it's an achievement you didn't have a moment ago.

So don't be shy about. Get some friends or family together- even if it's one other person and share your triumph. Allow yourself to feel the pleasure of moving one step forward to toward God's free gift of purpose to you.

This is no light thing, because Jesus didn't lend His breath to you in vain.

You've used His precious deposit of talents and the Holy Spirit and produced something that didn't exist before,
...something to serve your generation
...something to shape your culture
...something to beautify your surroundings
...something to pass on to your children
...something to advance the kingdom
...something to declare God's goodness
...something to leave a legacy of light behind.

This is much cause for celebration. Heaven and earth join with you to say "Well done good and faithful servant!"

You finished :)

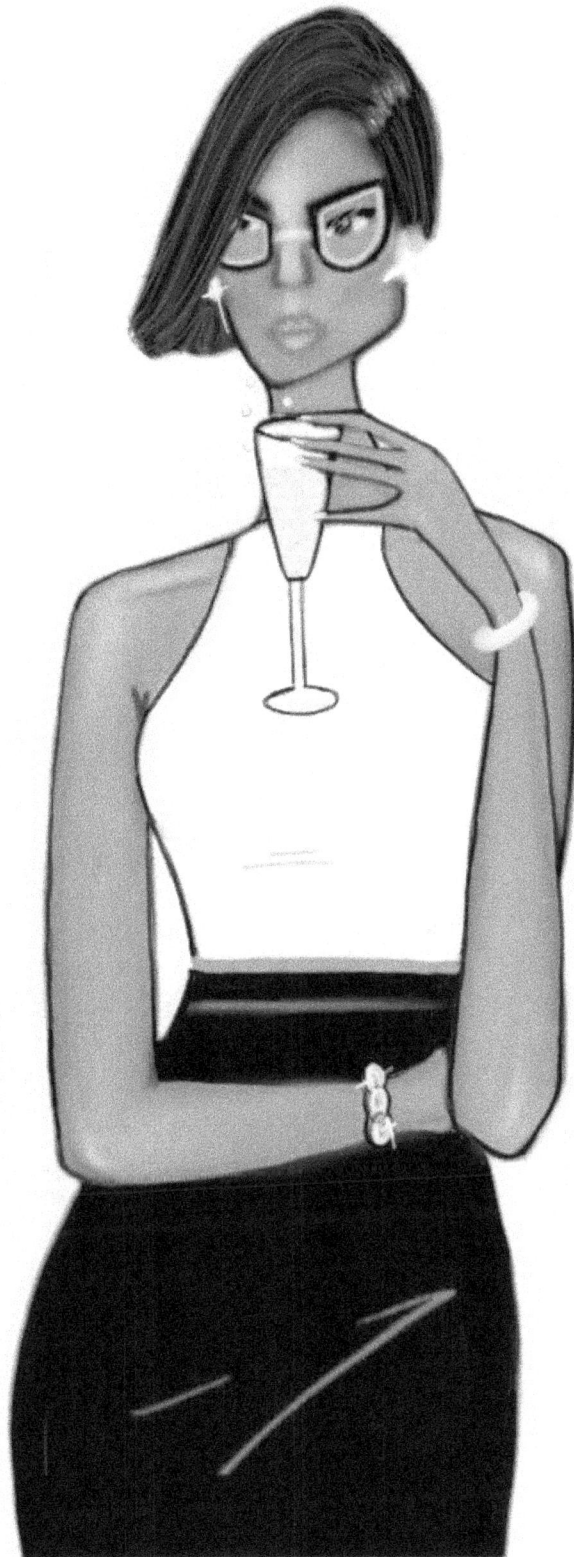

Our greatest fear should not be of failure, but of succeeding at things in life that don't really matter.

– Francis Chan

90
DAYS
TO
DONE!

TIME TO PLAN OUR WORK, SO WE CAN WORK OUR PLAN.

90 DAY PLANNER

BECAUSE DONE IS BETTER THAN PERFECT

MY RESOLUTION TO FINISH

(90 DAY COMMITMENT)

God has stirred my heart & asked me to create: (THE CALL)

So this quarter I will prioritize: (THE WHAT)

I need to finish this because: (THE WHY)

I cannot **make** time so I will **take** time from: (THE HOW)

I will set aside non-negotiable time to do this on: (THE WHEN)

To minimize distractions, I will go do this at: (THE WHERE)

To get accountability and snitch on my excuses, I will tell: (THE WHO)

Once this is done, I will finally feel: (THE WIN)

THIS QUARTER'S PROJECT:

I will complete _____ by _____

PROJECT DUMP: (LIST ALL POSSIBLE TASKS)

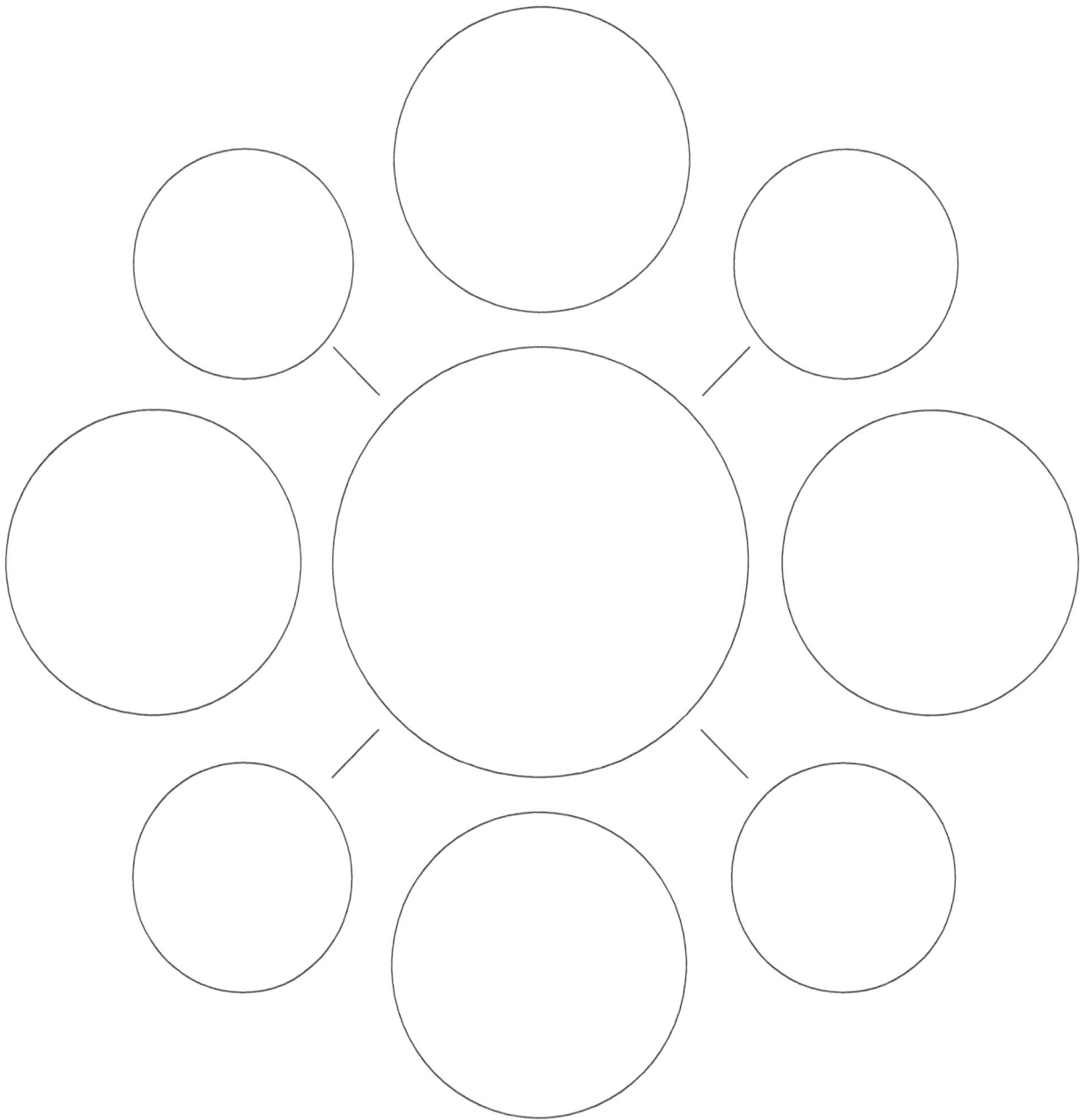

THIS QUARTER'S PRIORITIES (ASSIGN ESSENTIAL TASKS TO A SPECIFIC MONTH)

MONTH 1:

MONTH 2:

MONTH 3:

ITEMS TO FINISH FIRST:

1. _____

2. _____

3. _____

4. _____

5. _____

NOTES

_____

_____

_____

_____

_____

_____

Show me the way I should go, for to you I entrust my life.

Psalm 143:8

Month 1

SUNDAY	MONDAY	TUESDAY

WEDNESDAY	THURSDAY	FRIDAY	SATURDAY

THIS WEEK, I'M THANKFUL THAT I GET TO:

3 THINGS TO FINISH THIS WEEK:

MONDAY

PRIORITIES

TUESDAY

PRIORITIES

WEDNESDAY

PRIORITIES

FUEL TO FINISH: (PRAYERS, SCRIPTURE, MEMOS TO SELF...)

THURSDAY

PRIORITIES

FRIDAY

PRIORITIES

SATURDAY

SUNDAY

WEEKLY REFLECTION

HOW DID I FEEL ABOUT THIS WEEK?

ONE AMAZING THING THAT HAPPENED?

WHAT WILL I DO BETTER/DIFFERENTLY NEXT WEEK?

THINGS TO PRAY ABOUT (& NOT WORRY ABOUT)?

WHY DO I STILL NEED TO FINISH WHAT I STARTED?

NEW IDEAS, WISDOM, MINDSET SHIFTS:

_____

_____

_____

_____

_____

_____

_____

_____

_____

_____

_____

_____

_____

_____

_____

_____

_____

_____

THIS WEEK, I'M THANKFUL THAT I GET TO:

3 THINGS TO FINISH THIS WEEK:

MONDAY

PRIORITIES

TUESDAY

PRIORITIES

WEDNESDAY

PRIORITIES

FUEL TO FINISH: (PRAYERS, SCRIPTURE, MEMOS TO SELF…)

THURSDAY

PRIORITIES

FRIDAY

PRIORITIES

SATURDAY

SUNDAY

WEEKLY REFLECTION

HOW DID I FEEL ABOUT THIS WEEK?

ONE AMAZING THING THAT HAPPENED?

WHAT WILL I DO BETTER/DIFFERENTLY NEXT WEEK?

THINGS TO PRAY ABOUT (& NOT WORRY ABOUT)?

WHY DO I STILL NEED TO FINISH WHAT I STARTED?

NEW IDEAS, WISDOM, MINDSET SHIFTS:

_____

_____

_____

_____

_____

_____

_____

_____

_____

_____

_____

_____

_____

_____

_____

_____

_____

THIS WEEK, I'M THANKFUL THAT I GET TO:

3 THINGS TO FINISH THIS WEEK:

MONDAY

PRIORITIES

TUESDAY

PRIORITIES

WEDNESDAY

PRIORITIES

FUEL TO FINISH: (PRAYERS, SCRIPTURE, MEMOS TO SELF...)

THURSDAY

PRIORITIES

_____

_____

_____

_____

_____

FRIDAY

PRIORITIES

_____

_____

_____

_____

SATURDAY

SUNDAY

WEEKLY REFLECTION

HOW DID I FEEL ABOUT THIS WEEK?

ONE AMAZING THING THAT HAPPENED?

WHAT WILL I DO BETTER/DIFFERENTLY NEXT WEEK?

THINGS TO PRAY ABOUT (& NOT WORRY ABOUT)?

WHY DO I STILL NEED TO FINISH WHAT I STARTED?

NEW IDEAS, WISDOM, MINDSET SHIFTS:

_____

_____

_____

_____

_____

_____

_____

_____

_____

_____

_____

_____

_____

_____

_____

_____

THIS WEEK, I'M THANKFUL THAT I GET TO:

3 THINGS TO FINISH THIS WEEK:

MONDAY

PRIORITIES

_____

_____

_____

_____

TUESDAY

PRIORITIES

_____

_____

_____

_____

WEDNESDAY

PRIORITIES

_____

_____

_____

_____

FUEL TO FINISH: (PRAYERS, SCRIPTURE, MEMOS TO SELF...)

THURSDAY

PRIORITIES

_____
_____
_____
_____
_____

FRIDAY

PRIORITIES

_____
_____
_____
_____
_____

SATURDAY

SUNDAY

WEEKLY REFLECTION

HOW DID I FEEL ABOUT THIS WEEK?

ONE AMAZING THING THAT HAPPENED?

WHAT WILL I DO BETTER/DIFFERENTLY NEXT WEEK?

THINGS TO PRAY ABOUT (& NOT WORRY ABOUT)?

WHY DO I STILL NEED TO FINISH WHAT I STARTED?

NEW IDEAS, WISDOM, MINDSET SHIFTS:

_____

_____

_____

_____

_____

_____

_____

_____

_____

_____

_____

_____

_____

_____

_____

_____

_____

ITEMS TO FINISH FIRST:

1. _____

2. _____

3. _____

4. _____

5. _____

NOTES

_____

_____

_____

_____

_____

_____

"For I know the plans I have for you," declares the Lord.

Jeremiah 29:11

Month 2

SUNDAY	MONDAY	TUESDAY

WEDNESDAY	THURSDAY	FRIDAY	SATURDAY

THIS WEEK, I'M THANKFUL THAT I GET TO:

3 THINGS TO FINISH THIS WEEK:

MONDAY

PRIORITIES

TUESDAY

PRIORITIES

WEDNESDAY

PRIORITIES

FUEL TO FINISH: (PRAYERS, SCRIPTURE, MEMOS TO SELF...)

THURSDAY

PRIORITIES

_____
_____
_____
_____
_____

FRIDAY

PRIORITIES

_____
_____
_____
_____
_____

SATURDAY

SUNDAY

WEEKLY REFLECTION

HOW DID I FEEL ABOUT THIS WEEK?

ONE AMAZING THING THAT HAPPENED?

WHAT WILL I DO BETTER/DIFFERENTLY NEXT WEEK?

THINGS TO PRAY ABOUT (& NOT WORRY ABOUT)?

WHY DO I STILL NEED TO FINISH WHAT I STARTED?

NEW IDEAS, WISDOM, MINDSET SHIFTS:

_____

_____

_____

_____

_____

_____

_____

_____

_____

_____

_____

_____

_____

_____

_____

_____

_____

_____

_____

THIS WEEK, I'M THANKFUL THAT I GET TO:

3 THINGS TO FINISH THIS WEEK:

MONDAY

PRIORITIES

TUESDAY

PRIORITIES

WEDNESDAY

PRIORITIES

FUEL TO FINISH: (PRAYERS, SCRIPTURE, MEMOS TO SELF...)

THURSDAY

PRIORITIES

FRIDAY

PRIORITIES

SATURDAY

SUNDAY

WEEKLY REFLECTION

HOW DID I FEEL ABOUT THIS WEEK?

ONE AMAZING THING THAT HAPPENED?

WHAT WILL I DO BETTER/DIFFERENTLY NEXT WEEK?

THINGS TO PRAY ABOUT (& NOT WORRY ABOUT)?

WHY DO I STILL NEED TO FINISH WHAT I STARTED?

NEW IDEAS, WISDOM, MINDSET SHIFTS:

THIS WEEK, I'M THANKFUL THAT I GET TO:

3 THINGS TO FINISH THIS WEEK:

MONDAY

PRIORITIES

TUESDAY

PRIORITIES

WEDNESDAY

PRIORITIES

FUEL TO FINISH: (PRAYERS, SCRIPTURE, MEMOS TO SELF...)

THURSDAY

PRIORITIES

FRIDAY

PRIORITIES

SATURDAY

SUNDAY

WEEKLY REFLECTION

HOW DID I FEEL ABOUT THIS WEEK?

ONE AMAZING THING THAT HAPPENED?

WHAT WILL I DO BETTER/DIFFERENTLY NEXT WEEK?

THINGS TO PRAY ABOUT (& NOT WORRY ABOUT)?

WHY DO I STILL NEED TO FINISH WHAT I STARTED?

NEW IDEAS, WISDOM, MINDSET SHIFTS:

_____

_____

_____

_____

_____

_____

_____

_____

_____

_____

_____

_____

_____

_____

_____

_____

_____

_____

THIS WEEK, I'M THANKFUL THAT I GET TO:

3 THINGS TO FINISH THIS WEEK:

MONDAY

PRIORITIES

TUESDAY

PRIORITIES

WEDNESDAY

PRIORITIES

FUEL TO FINISH: (PRAYERS, SCRIPTURE, MEMOS TO SELF...)

THURSDAY

PRIORITIES

FRIDAY

PRIORITIES

SATURDAY

SUNDAY

WEEKLY REFLECTION

HOW DID I FEEL ABOUT THIS WEEK?

ONE AMAZING THING THAT HAPPENED?

WHAT WILL I DO BETTER/DIFFERENTLY NEXT WEEK?

THINGS TO PRAY ABOUT (& NOT WORRY ABOUT)?

WHY DO I STILL NEED TO FINISH WHAT I STARTED?

NEW IDEAS, WISDOM, MINDSET SHIFTS:

_____

_____

_____

_____

_____

_____

_____

_____

_____

_____

_____

_____

_____

_____

_____

_____

_____

Month **3**

1. _____

2. _____

3. _____

4. _____

5. _____

NOTES

_____

_____

_____

_____

_____

_____

_____

The mind of a man plans his way, but the Lord directs his steps.

Proverbs 16:9

SUNDAY	MONDAY	TUESDAY

WEDNESDAY	THURSDAY	FRIDAY	SATURDAY

THIS WEEK, I'M THANKFUL THAT I GET TO:

3 THINGS TO FINISH THIS WEEK:

MONDAY

PRIORITIES

TUESDAY

PRIORITIES

WEDNESDAY

PRIORITIES

FUEL TO FINISH: (PRAYERS, SCRIPTURE, MEMOS TO SELF...)

THURSDAY

PRIORITIES

_____

_____

_____

_____

_____

FRIDAY

PRIORITIES

_____

_____

_____

_____

_____

SATURDAY

SUNDAY

WEEKLY REFLECTION

HOW DID I FEEL ABOUT THIS WEEK?

ONE AMAZING THING THAT HAPPENED?

WHAT WILL I DO BETTER/DIFFERENTLY NEXT WEEK?

THINGS TO PRAY ABOUT (& NOT WORRY ABOUT)?

WHY DO I STILL NEED TO FINISH WHAT I STARTED?

NEW IDEAS, WISDOM, MINDSET SHIFTS:

_____

_____

_____

_____

_____

_____

_____

_____

_____

_____

_____

_____

_____

_____

_____

_____

_____

THIS WEEK, I'M THANKFUL THAT I GET TO:

3 THINGS TO FINISH THIS WEEK:

MONDAY

PRIORITIES

TUESDAY

PRIORITIES

WEDNESDAY

PRIORITIES

FUEL TO FINISH: (PRAYERS, SCRIPTURE, MEMOS TO SELF...)

THURSDAY

PRIORITIES

_____

_____

_____

_____

_____

FRIDAY

PRIORITIES

_____

_____

_____

_____

_____

SATURDAY

SUNDAY

WEEKLY REFLECTION

HOW DID I FEEL ABOUT THIS WEEK?

ONE AMAZING THING THAT HAPPENED?

WHAT WILL I DO BETTER/DIFFERENTLY NEXT WEEK?

THINGS TO PRAY ABOUT (& NOT WORRY ABOUT)?

WHY DO I STILL NEED TO FINISH WHAT I STARTED?

NEW IDEAS, WISDOM, MINDSET SHIFTS:

_____

_____

_____

_____

_____

_____

_____

_____

_____

_____

_____

_____

_____

_____

_____

THIS WEEK, I'M THANKFUL THAT I GET TO:

3 THINGS TO FINISH THIS WEEK:

MONDAY

PRIORITIES

TUESDAY

PRIORITIES

WEDNESDAY

PRIORITIES

FUEL TO FINISH: (PRAYERS, SCRIPTURE, MEMOS TO SELF...)

THURSDAY

PRIORITIES

_____

_____

_____

_____

_____

FRIDAY

PRIORITIES

_____

_____

_____

_____

_____

SATURDAY

SUNDAY

WEEKLY REFLECTION

HOW DID I FEEL ABOUT THIS WEEK?

ONE AMAZING THING THAT HAPPENED?

WHAT WILL I DO BETTER/DIFFERENTLY NEXT WEEK?

THINGS TO PRAY ABOUT (& NOT WORRY ABOUT)?

WHY DO I STILL NEED TO FINISH WHAT I STARTED?

NEW IDEAS, WISDOM, MINDSET SHIFTS:

THIS WEEK, I'M THANKFUL THAT I GET TO:

3 THINGS TO FINISH THIS WEEK:

MONDAY

PRIORITIES

TUESDAY

PRIORITIES

WEDNESDAY

PRIORITIES

FUEL TO FINISH: (PRAYERS, SCRIPTURE, MEMOS TO SELF...)

THURSDAY

PRIORITIES

FRIDAY

PRIORITIES

SATURDAY

SUNDAY

WEEKLY REFLECTION

HOW DID I FEEL ABOUT THIS WEEK?

ONE AMAZING THING THAT HAPPENED?

WHAT WILL I DO BETTER/DIFFERENTLY NEXT WEEK?

THINGS TO PRAY ABOUT (& NOT WORRY ABOUT)?

WHY DO I STILL NEED TO FINISH WHAT I STARTED?

NEW IDEAS, WISDOM, MINDSET SHIFTS:

_____

_____

_____

_____

_____

_____

_____

_____

_____

_____

_____

_____

_____

_____

_____

_____

_____

_____

WELL DONE, GOOD AND FAITHFUL SERVANT!

"But I do not account my life of any value nor as precious to myself, if only I may finish my course and the ministry that I received from the Lord Jesus, to testify to the gospel of the grace of God."

- Acts 20:24

Hey lionheart, you did it!

Be sure to check out **WomenWhoFinish.com**
for more planners, posters, podcasts and playbooks
to help you finish what you started this year.

It's been a joy to serve you.

Let's roar.

WOMEN WHO FINISH

YOU WERE SAVED TO IMPACT YOUR CULTURE. LEAD. SERVE. WIN.
YOUR VOICE WILL SOUND DIFFERENT. DO NOT BLEND IN. STAND OUT.
FOCUS ON YOUR CALLING. IT'S THE ONLY ONE YOU'LL BE GOOD AT.
JUST START. USE YOUR TALENTS. DREAM. ASK. THEN BELIEVE.
YOU WERE GIVEN THE VISION. SO YOU PURSUE IT. DO IT AFRAID.
OBEY. MAKE DISCIPLES. EXPECT THE SUPERNATURAL. EXECUTE.
LAY ONE BRICK TODAY. EXALT CHRIST. THEN GET EXALTED BY GOD.
KNOW YOUR WHY. SOLVE A PROBLEM. MAKE $$. CREATE BEAUTY.
FAIL OFTEN. GRACE WORKS. CHOOSE PROGRESS OVER PERFECTION.

PRIORITIZE YOUR PURPOSE. CELEBRATE YOUR WINS.

BUT FIRST, FINISH.

WomenWhoFinish.com

www.ingramcontent.com/pod-product-compliance
Lightning Source LLC
Chambersburg PA
CBHW081151090426
42736CB00017B/3279